VINE LINES

A humorous guide to wine terminology

Judy Valon

Illustrated by Roger Roberts

summersdale

VINE LINES
First published by CreativeVerve Australia in 2005.
This edition published in 2007 by Summersdale Publishers Ltd.
This edition copyright © Judy Valon and Roger Roberts, 2007.

Text by Judy Valon.
Illustrations by Roger Roberts.

Summersdale Publishers Ltd
46 West Street
Chichester
West Sussex
PO19 1RP
UK

www.summersdale.com

Printed and bound by Tien Wah Press, Singapore.

ISBN: 1-84024-552-2
ISBN 13: 978-1-84024-552-3

CONTENTS

Introduction...7

Enjoying Wine...10

Serving Wine..16

Fizz...39

White Wines..50

Red Wines...67

Dessert and Fortified Wines......................84

Port...86

Corked and Faulty Wines...........................88

Common Tasting Terms..............................91

Wine is life
Petronius, Roman writer

INTRODUCTION

Flabby, acidic, good nose, well constructed, citrus overtones, a hint of sweaty saddle… Wine lovers are skilled in conjuring up a myriad of scents and flavours with their discerning descriptions. This book explores the tasting vernacular in a light-hearted and humorous way.

The world has had a fascination with wine for thousands of years. Wine forms part of our everyday lives: we drink it to accompany fine and exotic foods; to celebrate a special event; to alleviate a stressful day at work; and sometimes we drink just because we want to and because we can! Whoever you are, wherever you are and whatever the occasion, there is a wine variety perfectly suited.

Only in the last twenty years have more of us taken a keen interest in the origins and quality of our wine. In this book we look at the bottle closure issue (cork vs screw cap); what constitutes a good wine; how long it should be laid down; what to drink with what; and countless other vine-related debates. This fun gift book is the perfect companion for any connoisseur in the making, whatever your preference or wine knowledge.

Traditionally wines are chosen to match certain foods; try a Pinot Noir with duck, a Shiraz with roast beef, a crisp and fruity Sauvignon Blanc with fish, or a sweet dessert wine accompanied by a wickedly indulgent dessert to fully enhance the dining experience.

However, you can drink any wine with any kind of food. There are elements of wine that will react to different kinds of food in different ways – these are essentially tannin, sugar, acid content and the alcohol level – but it all comes down to a personal choice and taste. Wine should be seen as an ingredient to social intercourse and all that is required to fully appreciate it is a reasonable sense of smell and taste and an interest in the many varieties available to us.

Wine undeniably provides pleasure and avid collectors enjoy investing money and time in their cellars. Whatever our budget or level of expertise, we nurture each bottle lovingly through its ageing process and fantasise about the special occasion when we will finally savour that unique drop.

Then truly comes the moment to let the wine terminology flow. This book is designed to give you a humorous interpretation of some of the most commonly uttered as well as the more obscure terms used to describe wines. 'Wine waffle', if you will, is bandied around to describe the smell, taste and aftertaste of this much-loved produce. Many terms have been illustrated to further assist you in making more 'intelligent' noises when in the company of the wine cognoscente.

We want this book to make you smile and derive even more pleasure from wine than you do today!

Cheers!

Mellow

ENJOYING WINE

Wine appeals to our senses of sight, smell and taste. From the design of the label and shape of the bottle to the colour of the wine in the glass, we are seduced. The popping of a champagne cork being pulled or the more subtle sigh of a wine cork, the first splash of wine poured, the first swill releasing its wonderful aromas – all attack our senses, arousing anticipation and desire.

Wine plays a major role in our social infrastructure – it's an indulgence, a mood enhancer and a stress reliever – and in moderation it has certain health advantages. Red wine has been reported to be full of antioxidants and can be effective in lowering the bad cholesterol which can lead to cardiovascular disease. More recently, discoveries have shown that antioxidants in white wine could be more effective than those in red. To be safe, drink both!

The varieties available and their often complex descriptions may seem daunting but remember, there are no rules when it comes to wine appreciation. Learning more about wine is easy: the Internet, of course, is a great source of information; take a wine tour as your next holiday; enter any of the thousands of cellar doors throughout the world and speak with their knowledgeable staff. Try different grape styles and producers. A good wine producer and indeed wine shop are invaluable in giving advice and assisting us in making a good choice.

Wine regions are some of the most beautiful parts of the world, so get out there and visit them.

Life is too short to drink bad wine
Anonymous

long and lean

laying it down

bottle-aged

Approachable at a Younger Age

SOME BASIC RULES OF THUMB FOR
SERVING WINE

Pre-lunch or pre-dinner drinks: Sherry, champagne or sparkling wine, lighter style white wines (red wine is better served with food). These are regarded as appetite stimulants and are perfect served with olives, nuts or light nibbles.

During the meal: Commence with the lighter style wines to accompany an entrée (whites or a light red), moving on to a heavier-bodied wine for the main course.

To serve with dessert, you cannot surpass a luscious sweet or fortified wine, such as a spatlese or botrytis Riesling.

To round off the meal, with perhaps some cheese and for total indulgence, there are exquisite fortified wines such as muscat, Madeira or port.

Bon appetit!

She gets to keep the chalet and the Rolls,
I want the Montrachet

Anonymous, *Forbes* magazine, 6 May 1996

bacon Character

horizontal tasting

distinctive nose

Powerful

I drink it when I'm happy and when I'm sad. Sometimes I drink it when I'm alone. When I have company I consider it obligatory. I trifle with it if I'm not hungry and I drink it when I am. Otherwise I never touch it, unless I'm thirsty

Madame Lily Bollinger

Burgundy makes you think of silly things, Bordeaux makes you talk of them and champagne makes you do them

Jean-Anthelme Brillat-Savarin

There are only two occasions when I drink Champagne, and these are: when I have game for dinner and when I haven't

Attributed to S. D. Churchill

tightly wound

full-bodied

long and silky

extra kick from the Oak

In victory, you deserve Champagne,
in defeat, you need it

Napoleon Bonaparte

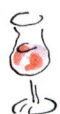

I cook with wine; sometimes I even add it to the food

W. C. Fields

Wine is the most civilized thing in the world

Ernest Hemingway

lithe and elegant

Youthful Aromas

Shows Promise

hollow

Mature

Volatile

Well balanced

Structured and Chewy

*If your heart is warm with happiness, you'll need a glass
— if sorrow chills your heart, have two*

Lehmusvuori Hannu

*What though youth gave love and roses,
age still leaves us friends and wine*

Thomas Moore

Wine is bottled poetry

Robert Louis Stevenson

light-bodied

high Acidity

fun and frivolous

FIZZ

Champagne, sparkling wine, fizz or bubbles – wherever a cork is popped, there is an uplifting, celebratory feeling; whether it is for a special event, served as an aperitif, sipped with an indulgent breakfast… or just because!

Methode traditionelle, the classic procedure for making champagne, is essentially a secondary fermentation inside the bottle after sugar and yeast are added to the wine. This produces further alcohol and creates the wonderful sparkles. The bottles are then aged from six months to three years before being put on lees (sur lie), where they are turned daily to keep the sediment in contact with the cork. To complete the process a small amount of liquid in the bottle neck is frozen and then disgorged along with the sediment before the bottle is re-corked and secured with a wire cage. This traditional process creates wonderful toasty, yeasty and fruity flavours.

The above method is, of course, very labour intensive and takes years. More economical ways, such as carbonation, have been developed to produce a finished sparkling wine in months, though they lack the romance of the longer, old-fashioned methode traditionelle.

There is a large range of both white and red sparkling wines that are kinder on the wallet, which means we can drink them more regularly. Bubbles are perfect for breakfast, lunch and dinner – and any time in between!

barnyard

Creamy

earthy

Perfumed

Chocolate

Wine... the intellectual part of the meal

Alexander Dumas

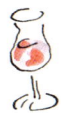

Good wine is a necessity of life for me

Thomas Jefferson

Penicillin cures but wine makes people happy

Sir Alexander Fleming

truffle

Strawberry lift

toasty

Well developed

WHITE WINES

When buying a white wine today, you can choose between many different blends and varieties from around the world. The traditional Riesling and Chardonnay have been joined by relatively new kids on the shelf such as Semillon, Viognier and Pinot Gris, and the list continues to grow as the smaller vineyards search for new markets for their alternative varieties. White wines tend towards fruit flavours, including hints of citrus, apple, pear, apricot, lychee and gooseberry; with occasional vegetable flavours such as asparagus, capsicum and herbaceous tones. They are often aromatic with distinct herbal and floral scents and even sometimes a tinge of freshly cut grass.

Fruity dry white wines are food friendly go well with many different kinds of food, are easy on the palate and delightful to drink on their own.

Let us have wine and women, mirth and laughter.
Sermons and soda water the day after

Lord Byron *(Don Juan)*

buttery

dusty

Shows bubblegum

tart

Wine improves with age – I like it more the older I get

Unknown

I have enjoyed great health at a great age, because every day since I can remember, I have consumed a bottle of wine except when I have not felt well. Then I have consumed two bottles

Attributed to a Bishop of Seville

herbaceous

harmony

Sweet floral nose

fig

Charred

Quickly, bring me a beaker of wine, so that I may wet my mind and say something clever

Aristophanes

When I read about the evils of drinking, I gave up reading

Henny Youngman

Men are like wine – some turn to vinegar, but the best improve with age

Pope John XXIII

dry finish

gooseberry

freshly cut grass

floral bouquet

Oozing Apricot

RED WINES

Reds have been described as more suited to the mature palate; the more experienced drinker is better able to identify and appreciate the complex variety of rich flavours.

Reds can vary from the lighter styles through to the seriously full-bodied aged varieties with muscle. The latter need more care and attention when storing but such efforts can be exceptionally rewarding. Mostly reds are served at room temperature and if allowed to breathe a little, the result is a deeply flavoursome drink – from a lighter style Pinot Noir with its wonderful earthy aromas and the lesser known Italian variety Nebbiolo, through to a smooth and easy-to-drink Merlot. Whether you choose the popular Cabernet Sauvignon with its dark fruit flavours, the lighter style Cabernet Franc, a perfumed Grenache or a heavier, spicy yet full-of-fruit Shiraz, all of these varieties are best served with food and can be enjoyed at informal barbecues and formal dinner parties alike. They are great partners to everything from sausages to casseroles to the family roast, and make excellent companions to hard cheeses.

The flavours and aromas in red wines are more intense, as are the tannins which can cause allergic reactions in a few of us. You will experience red soft fruits – e.g. cherry, plum, blackcurrant, blackberry, strawberry and raspberry – and sometimes you will notice chocolate and smoky tobacco tones. Most heavier style red wines will benefit from cellaring for a few years to develop their characteristics to the full.

Wine makes every meal an occasion,
every table more elegant, every day more civilised

Andre Simon

a complex little red

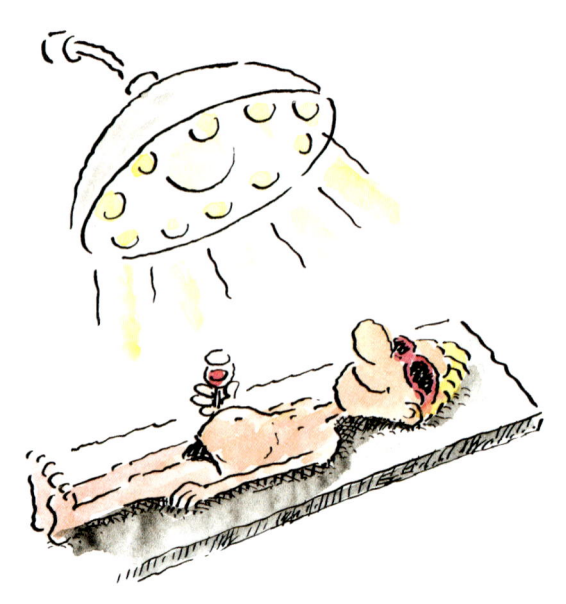

tannin

Coffee

beetroot

Plum Pudding

brooding intensity

Compromises are for relationships, not wine

Sir Robert Scott Caywood

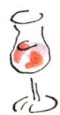

Wine makes daily living easier, less hurried, with fewer tensions and more tolerance

Benjamin Franklin

My only regret in life is that I did not drink more Champagne

John Maynard Keynes

f l a b b y

A hint of sweaty saddle

Cigar box Overtones

firm Structure

Sometimes when I reflect back on all the wine I drink, I feel shame. Then I look into the glass and think about the workers in the vineyards and all of their hopes and dreams. If I didn't drink this wine, they might be out of work and their dreams would be shattered.
Then I say to myself, 'It is better that I drink this wine and let their dreams come true, rather than be selfish and worry about my liver.'

Jack Handy

Meaty

leathery brute

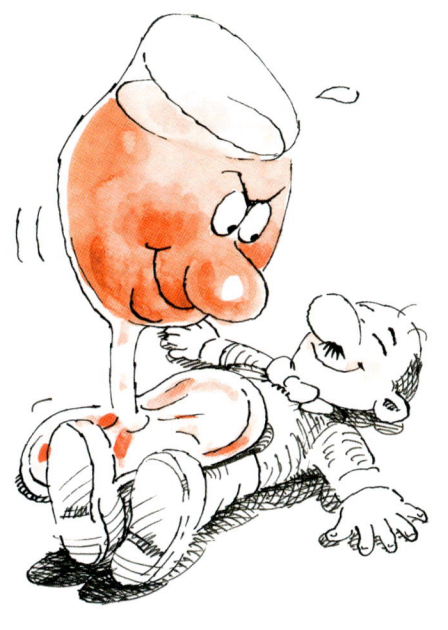

a heavy red

DESSERT AND FORTIFIED WINES

The golden and honey-like dessert wines are created by grapes shrivelled on the vine by a mould known as 'noble rot' or botrytis. This shrivelling process intensifies the sugars and, served well chilled, the resulting wine is a perfectly delicious end to a meal, accompanied by fruit, desserts or soft cheeses. These wines will age well for several years… if you can leave them alone!

Late-picked varieties (known as spatlese) can be served in a similar way but the flavours are not as intensely concentrated.

Sherry, fortified with brandy, is the perfect aperitif. Invented by the Spanish around the southern town of Jerez, it is the perfect companion to tapas and nibbles. However, sherry is often misunderstood and unappreciated. The market has been flooded with sickly-sweet imitations which in fact bear no resemblance to a refined and traditional sherry. True sherries take years to produce and take their complexity from ageing and blending. They should be served well chilled and are ideal appetite whetters. Just remember the alcohol content is high at 15 per cent or more.

fortified

PORT

Port is a sweet, strong wine originating in Portugal, mostly made from red grapes though a smaller amount of white port is also made from white grapes. The wine is made by adding brandy during fermentation, which stops the process before its completion. Port is then matured in wood before being bottled. The liquid is originally of a ruby hue and, after ageing in wood for five years, loses its intensity of colour to become tawny. An 'aged tawny' has been aged in wood for a longer period.

Port is an after-dinner drink served with cheese or dessert and traditionally belonged to the male domain, though these days men and women alike enjoy its rich, heady properties.

If food is the body of good living, wine is its soul

Clifton Fadiman

Noble rot

CORKED AND FAULTY WINES

An impression of mothballs, burnt matches or being stewed, or lack of fruit flavours on the nose or palate are all signs of faulty wines. They could be the result of storing at an inappropriate temperature, an excess of sulphur in the wine-making process, 'cork taint' or oxidation. Fortunately, the proportion of wines that are faulty is very low, but here are the most common causes to be on the lookout for:

Corked: When the wine becomes tainted with mould that develops in the cork producing a damp, mouldy smell that totally dominates the bouquet of the wine. When choosing a wine with a cork, you should always check that the cork is flush with the bottle neck and not protruding. With the advent of the Stelvin screw cap and the new generation synthetic corks, this problem will become less common.

Oxidation: This occurs when the wine receives too much oxygen and subsequently produces a stale smell and taste and brownish discolouration of the wine.

Sulphur: This is a commonly used preservative; used judiciously it will stabilise the wine both during the wine-making process and afterwards. However, excessive use will produce unpleasant flavours and aromas.

Volatile: This term refers to the effect created when the acetic acid levels are too high and produce a wine with a pungent, dominating aroma that is sharp and sour – think vinegar and nail polish remover.

Corked

COMMON TASTING TERMS

aromatic	Distinctive floral or herb nose: Riesling, Pinot Gris, Viognier and Sauvignon Blanc
biscuity	Champagne methode traditionelle
body	Texture: light, medium or full
buttery	Champagne methode traditonelle, Chardonnay
complex	Multi-dimensional flavours (potential for ageing)
creamy	Champagne
crisp	Light young white wines
dry	Wines whose final flavour in the mouth is dry
earthy	Extra depth of fruit: Cabernet Sauvignon, Shiraz
finish	The end flavour of the wine
floral	Gewurtztraminer and Riesling
gamey	Mature red wines: Pinot Noir, Shiraz
herbaceous	Leafy and aromatic: Sauvignon Blanc
leathery	Think horse saddle: aged Pinot Noir and Shiraz
length	The lingering aftertaste
nutty	Aged Semillion: Chardonnay
oaky	Matured in oak: Chardonnay
peppery	Spicy, freshly ground black pepper: Shiraz
spicy	Peppery, aromatic wines: Riesling, Pinot Gris, Shiraz and Grenache
structure	The combination of fruit, acid and tannin tastes
tannin	Mainly in reds, the dry chalkiness
yeasty	As for 'creamy' and 'biscuity': champagne styles

rich and Concentrated

fruit cake

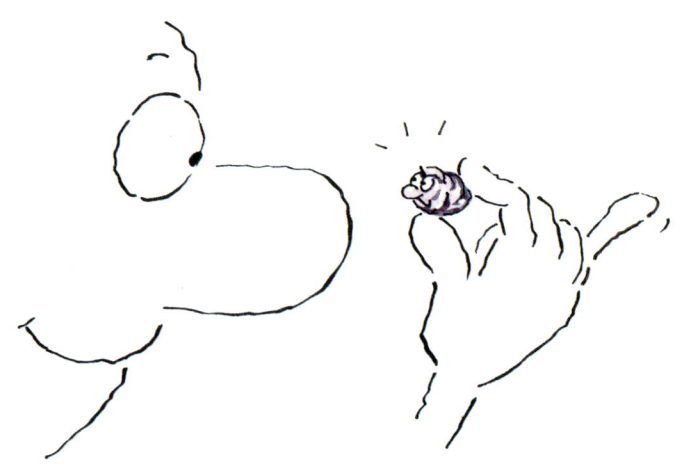

intense currant

(At his first sip of champagne)
Come quickly, I am tasting stars

Dom Perignon

www.summersdale.com